Still

poems by

Nathalie E. Amazan

Finishing Line Press
Georgetown, Kentucky

Still

Copyright © 2023 by Nathalie E. Amazan
ISBN 979-8-88838-289-9 First Edition
All rights reserved under International and Pan-American Copyright Conventions. No part of this book may be reproduced in any manner whatsoever without written permission from the publisher, except in the case of brief quotations embodied in critical articles and reviews.

ACKNOWLEDGMENTS

Thank you to Finishing Line Press for giving me the opportunity to publish my first chapbook. Thank you to Sazia Patel for the guidance, encouragement, and love. Thank you to all my family, mentors, and friends that have pushed me to develop my craft. A huge thanks to my brother from another mother—Ethan K. Bherwani who departed this Earth on May 27, 2021. Ethan always believed in my greatest potential, and I hope this chapbook lived up to his expectations. Above all, all praise and thanks are for Allah, The Light for giving me this gift of writing poetry. I pray I use this gift to the best of my abilities and for the best of outcomes, Ameen.

Publisher: Leah Huete de Maines
Editor: Christen Kincaid
Cover Art: Sazia Patel
Author Photo: Sazia Patel
Cover Design: Elizabeth Maines McCleavy

Order online: www.finishinglinepress.com
also available on amazon.com

Author inquiries and mail orders:
Finishing Line Press
PO Box 1626
Georgetown, Kentucky 40324
USA

Table of Contents

January 1st 1

On top of boulders, a green sea hovers 2

Still (I) 3

When We Get There 4

An-Nur (The Light) 7

Still (IV) 8

Hiatus 9

Comfort 11

Prior Nights 12

UN Photos 13

Still (II) 14

the 2 joints 15

Love Poem 16

Still (III) 21

May 22

Trees are a mercy 23

Intertwined 24

January 1st

Its Jumu'ah.*
We pray for Liberation in all Its forms;
Her Breath is felt
as wind
brings a bird over water waves
        echo calmness
through your frigid sun lit fist
my fingers find valleys for refuge.
Earth may be at its precipice,
tangled we'll make it through the circumference
grasping onto Truth.
We rest,
surrounded by no one who knows our names,
sharing intimacy
between Webster Ave and Puritan Street
        what do our contradictions mean?
Peace is in these moments
through movements of mass
moving towards us
while we stand
on rocks sturdy enough for our feet.
The sun has ascended:
thus, with perspective, today may be a start.
A precipice could be a promise of good times to come
so, We pray for Liberation in all Its forms
even if it means no longer seeing the sunrise from this place anymore.

Jumu'ah: Friday; a sacred day of worship in the Islamic tradition. This is the day for mid-day congregational prayers.

On top of boulders, a green sea hovers

On top of boulders, a green sea hovers.
Unsettled silence accompanies us.
Blues merge into yellow hues and flowers
droop in bunches upon themselves, and thus
swells life into our soles. Rest in water
black birds' angel-stretched wings swim, float in ease.
We, a Brother and Sister lay, wonder:
        How beautiful they must feel, constant peace.
Their breeze is our shade, our praise nourishment.
These bees bring memorable melodies,
smoke in the distance noticed by eye squint—
A soundless beetle hides, crawls onto me.

We, Brother and Sister, hike up and down
sharing quiet outside the busy town.

Still (I)

Weeping upon maroon shoulders
reminiscent of ancestors
kin   kith   skin.
Since love is all we ever wanted, we will find it;
no ultimatums.
Strategies for survival are inevitable in bondage.

When We Get There

Question everything.
Struggle in the present for the world we wish to live in
accept tragedy as inevitable
like laughter of healing
pain is unavoidable
truth is coming at roots
lifting liberation from twisted tongues
forcing mother out for colonizers' boots to drag into our homes
us out onto ships of wet bones,
cold trails,
graveyards,
one in the same;
they were not invited
but we are a hospitable people who
embody the teachings of Jesus (pbuh) better than any church on
stolen land could ever even begin to think of what it could mean to
love a neighbor without exception,
we clean feet of our guests
empty cabinets for their sustenance
we understand life is sacred
we exist in community
with the inalienable rights of air, water, land, and the heavens;
know where you come from,
who you come from?
know the emotions that color your veins
blending yesterday into today where
past is future is past and present and forever is non-linear
don't be discouraged if the peculiarities of tomorrow signify
regression
we are more than our present circumstances,
freedom without imagination is emptier than good without love
freedom without freedom is too often the cause of destruction
if you're not writing for freedom,
what are you doing then?
free your soul
free the world
siege on Gaza dripping blood in the sea

blowing secondhand ash into the river
have you heard the tear-gassed screams coming out of Falesteen?
Can't breathe!
not enough ventilators for the children growing up in open air prisons
plantations of legal exploitation
history doesn't repeat
just keeps going on till we do something different
What does it mean to no longer feel state violence?
What is a state?
Who owns violence?
What is my body if I cannot identify it?
Who am I really besides a kid too scared to sleep so never fails my dreams of reaching peace of the holy land of revolution where we can be whatever we wanna be without being scared to sleep without working lungs out dry,
worry about blood pressure getting too high or
how to survive the next day's rent or
demolition
where Michael's still living
Ahmed is married
Trayvon's flying on the moon with an airplane and
Sandra is President;
where return to land of who we come from is an expectation
where trauma no longer carries the magnitude of air inescapable as breath
where I do not cry writing a poem I don't know if I can see the future of—
I'm young and
alive,
so how can I be a pessimist?
Baldwin, take the wheel
take my hand,
guide me towards the land of the holiest revolution
of love liberated from suffering
suffocated by human beings scared of their death so they made us to hate and divide

trying to conquer life is impossible
didn't they know
spirit never dies
trying to conquer life is impossible
didn't you know
spirit never dies
don't we know spirit never dies
we got centuries of warriors living
when we look into our eyes
ain't starting from scratch
got foundations of tradition
innovation
taste
rhythm
empathy as community ethic
past is future is past and present and forever is non-linear
don't you remember?
spirit never dies
spirit never dies
spirit never dies
don't you forget
when we get there.

An-Nur (The Light)

At nightfall, our feet march over martyrs
whose bodies in soil produce our growth,
where bloodied bullets in children slaughtered—
Living on the landscapes of death, I'm told
of just wars; of justice in righteous sin,
despite this, the olive trees grew again.
I choose to listen to intuition,
it's been written in the stars God has sent
wailing: we will be free no matter what.
Though war may make us part for now we will
form community out of gorgeous stuff:
a compassionate love on Earth we'll fill.

Our tongues will lift to break what is not right.
Our hands, our hearts will guide with written Light.

Still (IV)

Living in bedrooms
looking out at avenues
ashed feet from a day's salah*
maroon cloth in wash
I do nothing but watch.

**Salah: Prayer*

Hiatus

Being human is not easy to do even if you're dead.
The complexity of decomposition and
intricacy of withering bones deteriorating
is only an aspect of this human life
not quite defined
yet
still I
take the time to
make sense of these lines
on this paper of mine

stop
midline
I don't know what to write next.

But, You glide my hand from left to right
reminding me:
        breaks are fine,
            just do not neglect to start again.

Again, I left You for awhile
I would love to say
I don't know why
thoughts echo otherwise
        do not loose meaning in life, said I
sad I, pick up this pen
turning empty pages of
would have been
could have been
should have been
clever statements and words mix matched
formed in a melodic syntax
verbs, nouns, adjectives
acting as additives in this never-ending narrative of
damages felt from a break too many.

But, You then glide my hand from left to right
whispering calmly
like You always do:
> breaks are fine,
> just do not neglect to start again.

Again, I make stupid excuses
in the hopes of excusing my unwillingness to come back
ignoring that
Our energies were essentially made to complement
and make sense of each other
when no one else was, You were
the fact of the matter is,
You make me happy.

You remind me that beauty may not just be in the eye of the
beholder
rather,
in the hands of those willing to capture it down
on this paper
everlasting evolving with me
eternally waiting to be inked
I can't think of being away from You again.

You should never hear this pen of mine pop from the end
like I have finished the end of this poem;
poems do not end
instead, they bend
through time and space
manipulating seconds, minutes, and lyrical sentences
until it's

Comfort

Solace and Silence
On Stoops and Stairwells reveal
Truths about Ourselves.

Prior Nights

I've walked
holding onto Life
with tears like rain
regenerates
creates streams
sliding down our cheeks
foundations for greens, to breathe.
Eventually they dry,
it all dries
and we are here all over again,
letting go
holding onto Truth
of change: Life and Death.

    I hope after we danced and laughed
    we tried to answer why
    he empties bottles from the trash
    adding to mountains soon exchanged for cash
    unaffected by strangers' cheers
    the plaza is lit!
    a cello and voice tune to join symphonies of impromptu music
    while police move forward as if cued
    it is truly scenic.
    I wonder,
    about the tears in children's eyes
    about the soldier that dies
    will complacency be the end of me?

I'm holding onto questions
letting go of fabricated unity
while moving my body to the
                off
                          beat
    band
creating Life by water;
he passes me magic
under lilac (diesel) skies
as we try to find reasons to smile tomorrow night.

UN Photos

I do not know feet without calluses
stomach emptier than hearts of so-called saviors
slaughtered my mother
claimed I'm no longer theirs—
Why the hell is he taking my picture?

Still (II)

everything has its time
everything is everything
all the time
nothing is something too
empty void space got some energy too.
Isn't a Black universe just a vacuum?
Isn't a "Black" being just a phantom,
a fantasy
strangling our empathy.
Isn't a poem just my way of forming tears in letters of a language
to reach your ears when stars light up just enough to catch the
corner of my cornea clearly seeing our souls of Love as Light
surrounds us—
isn't a poem just selfish?
isn't it healing too?

The 2 joints

between the two of us
watching stars amazed they made it
past tall lights of buildings
surround our bodies.
On that night
with the 2 joints between the two of us
could you notice my body?
How it moved at your shuffling towards or away
lying back down
hair spread
knees up
feet grounded
on our turf;
did you notice my body?
Slowing dragging out
smoke between puffs
I wondered: did you notice us?

> The 2 joints
> between the two of us is a break
> from confusion,
> unquestioned tradition.

My heart bled its shame
when the two joints between
our lips faded away.

Love Poem

My grandmother is in a casket.
we can't stop lashing out,
I'm sad n' shit.
                l-o-v-e.

        lost
                                  how you really feel?"

    resentful

for a second

      embarrassed

    damn
You are comfortable in
        discomfort sometimes
      I exist

Your hairs
not tied back
fly
forward

hands extend for the body you thought
lost
how transient being is.

And when my body dies, it may become a number of things
like free.

I can't write a love poem.
If I can find comfort closest to colonial convention,
then maybe
my soul could be saved from Hell
built by conquest
neither an abomination
nor the weak rib
perhaps, proving to myself my possibility to exist.

Do you really want a love poem?
I mean, the earth is on fire and
melting ice sheets are rising over the city
will we ever be able to breathe
if the atmosphere continues to choke us out into the cracks
in the dirt of the pavement
deaf to our pleas of 'I can't breathe'
so basically, I no longer fall in love
cuz,
it may be catastrophically devastating.
The city is burning while drowning
and I love contradictions more than Whitman.

What a cliché: a sad love story
are you kidding me?
I'm already Gen Z
meaning we're weird
we use memes to communicate
death is a punchline
      I guess it's like a part of evolution or something
But, love?
You really gotta be kidding me!
It seems foolish to discuss love *w/o talking abt* racism *which seems foolish to discuss w/o talking abt* white supremacy *which seems foolish to discuss w/o talking abt* insecurity
We're #woke like that.
    "Woke"
    "Love"
    "Poetry"
More specifically,
I can't write a love poem
cuz, I am not angry
enough.

I'm turning over to see my greatest nightmare stare right back
empty n'
off white n'
nothing n'
glaring
waiting
for truth
or something of the sort;
air is thick
like through pauses
silences
breath
eye movements
      look at these birds moving in packs making space for the
little ones to survive
I digress.

I learn growth by the intensity of the sun
how it cannot be stared at for too long as if it is purity
maybe it is
maybe it isn't
who cares?
we all are and aren't always
you are and aren't always
anyways
we're in our 20s
we're kids barely
why do we believe love can only exist for one person one way at a time
have we lost all imagination?
what is forever if not just the present moment?

You say: Break my heart, that takes courage.
I say: I love you.
But, this is not a love poem all
cliché n' shit all
normal n' shit all
boring n' shit all
not my style n' shit
but, shit—
We are the U-Haul I vowed my closeted teen self to never become.

My full body must catch my tongue before I let the truth roll out with no filter
        I love the way you roll our spliffs,
and no
this is still not a love poem
but, I can use the word "love" all I want
cuz, I said so.
This is my poem
a testimony of love beyond force.
I do not have the courage to break a thing, a being;
I am not as radical as you may think
my pen is the closest I've been to revolution.

I
am
stuck
on
the Break
trying
to make
pleasing art of syllables in sentences
pages over
I got lost
stopped
picked you up
took you
nowhere
moving on n' on
until there is
was something
no guarantees.

I may be scared without you
Is that not love too?

Call it stubbornness wants
following my own fate
or simply
using the erotic as power within my life.

I can no longer try to find words to put into form;
perhaps, this is something like a love poem.

Still (III)

When I'm gone from sight, say just my name.
There's no worship for bones
only remembrance of souls;
speak of ways we embraced beyond torsos of clay
enjoy how sun rises for me.
Sleep, please don't forget me.

May

My fingers kick the dirt that engulfs You.
Instead of lain roses, we plant sage here.
My body on top of your Home is nude:
today I choose to not cover any tear.
A porch waits across for us to sit on,
Your mom digs her eyes into mine as if
I am an artifact of her lost son
who drowned with air flowing between his lips—
You became a cliché upon that bed:
A lifeless copy of your smile cracked,
tubes and machines circling round your head.
The notice came, I fell on knees, hunchbacked.

A tornado swirled me up those past days.
Now no longer do flowers bloom in May.

Trees are a mercy

Trees are a mercy. Buckets of soft ice
held as cover; they whisper: I got' chu.
    I know we're not the best of friends, but I
    feel your breath shake, back and forth your bones move.
    You don't have to hide from me or yourself.
    I understand, the tension in the land
    hurts me too. For more years than you could guess
    I've seen families turn to guests then
    strangers, separated by fake borders:
    they all are. These roots stretch centuries back
    when we needed less, mostly each other
    and nature was balanced, smelled of lilacs.

    I tell you these things, my dear don't forget.
    Only few can hear now, write what I've said.

Intertwined

I am not only a moment,
I am all the moments that were, that are, and will be,
I transcend these three to somewhere…
something of a beautiful and spiritual dimension we all know.
The way the bitternut hickory greens as it sings in the beginning of the
March season, brings me its peace;
and as the ocean rises and falls, my soul moves along with her,
because we have known each other before I was born.
Each ascending sunrise followed by the descending sunset, with distinct
coalesced shades;
The insects that bring life to these plants,
These plants that bring life to me
Beautiful cycle of humanity, this is the constitution of my anatomy.
The motion of these waves I stand before, are the reason for my heartbeat,
The gentle air hugging my body whispers oxygen to my lungs,
and I listen to it move swiftly down the path they've made, and I think:
"How beautifully elegant."
Thoreau has become a part of me;
"Simplicity, simplicity, simplicity," these simple things are of me.
The laughter of my mother,
Ambition of my father,
The awe-filled defiant natures of my brother and sister
each are inscribed on the neurons transmitted throughout my body,
They come to make their home and color my DNA.
The reflection I see of myself
shows Saturn's rings circulating this body of mine in all its glory,
Pluto's newfound majesty in my own eyes,
And stardust exhaling like a cloud from my breath.
I am Water that keeps me live,
I am Fire that burns deep,
I am Earth that reminds me of my composition,
I am Air I inhale,
In all moments, I am.

NOTES

The lines "*about the tears in children's eyes / about the soldier that dies*" in "Prior Nights" are from Rodriguez's song, "I Wonder."
The line "*under lilac (diesel) skies*" in "Prior Nights" is from Timmy Sullivan's poem, "In Prospect Park We're Gonna Cry Some Tears Tonight."

The line "*everything is everything*" in Still (II) is from noname's songs "All I Need" and "Forever" who is quoting Lauryn Hill's song "Everything Is Everything."

"Love Poem" is inspired by Tommy Pico's *Nature Poem*. The lines "*And when my body dies, it may become a number of things*" and "*It seems foolish to discuss ... w/o talking abt ... / which seems foolish to discuss w/o talking abt ... / which seems foolish to discuss w/o talking abt ...* " are from *Nature Poem*.

A slightly different version of "When We Get There" was published in *Falastin Magazine,* Volume 4, Issue 3 (2020) by the Palestinian American Community Center. and in *Poetic Justice: An Anthology of Poems by Muslims* (2022) by Strange Inc. Press.

A slightly different version of "Intertwined" and "Love Poem" were published in the *Jabberwocky* Undergraduate Literary Journal by the UMass Amherst English Department (2018 and 2020).

Nathalie E. Amazan is a Haitian American poet and writer from New York. Nathalie's writing strives to move people to recognize the power within our souls to create more peaceful and loving ways of being. When Nathalie was 17, she was a Grand Champion of the Walt Whitman Birthplace Association Poetry Contest. Since then, she has shared poems and performed in several venues such as the Nuyorican Poets Café where she was a Wednesday Night Slam winner. Her poems have appeared in Button Poetry's 2021 Video Contest, the *Jabberwocky Undergraduate Literary Journal* at UMass Amherst and other online and in print publications. Find some of her writings and connect with her @natamazan on all online platforms.

www.ingramcontent.com/pod-product-compliance
Lightning Source LLC
Chambersburg PA
CBHW022128090426
42743CB00008B/1055